**Compiled, Written and Edited by:**
Katie Read
**Design, Illustrations and Layout:**
Isobel Kinnear
**Series Editor:** Simon Melhuish

Published by Lagoon Books
UK: PO Box 58528, London SW13 3AY
USA: 10685-B Hazelhurst Dr. #9988
Houston, TX77043

Printed in China

ISBN: 978-1-90281-381-3

www.thelagoongroup.com

# TRIVIA
## FOR THE TOILET

**?**

# Catnip can affect lions and tigers.

Fingernails grow nearly four times faster than toenails.

Istanbul is the only city located on two continents

In Susami Bay in Japan, there's a postbox 10 metres underwater.

The 'philtrum,' the indent between your nose and lips, was considered erotic by Ancient Romans. They called it "Cupid's Bow."

**?**

A group of unicorns is called a blessing.

Right-handers live on average nine years longer than left-handers.

# Spider blood is transparent, but technically blue.

The most common pub name in the UK is 'The Red Lion'.

*Surprisingly, your brain is more active at night than during the day.*
*Also, people with higher IQs dream more.*

**?**

7% OF THE ENTIRE IRISH BARLEY CROP GOES INTO GUINNESS.

*The giant squid has the largest eyes in the world.*

THE CAN-OPENER WAS INVENTED 48 YEARS AFTER THE CAN.

FEMALE APHIDS ARE OFTEN BORN PREGNANT, AND MALES DO NOT EVEN EXIST IN SOME APHID SPECIES.

# 40% of women admit to throwing footwear at men.

**?**

*The Muppet Show was banned in Saudi Arabia because of Miss Piggy.*

LIGHT DOESN'T ALWAYS TRAVEL AT THE SPEED OF LIGHT. IT HAS BEEN RECORDED MOVING AS SLOWLY AS 38MPH.

THE DOORS WERE NAMED AFTER ALDOUS HUXLEY'S HALLUCINOGEN-ENDORSING BOOK, 'THE DOORS OF PERCEPTION'. IN TURN, HUXLEY'S WORK, IS A REFERENCE TO THE WILLIAM BLAKE QUOTE: "IF THE DOORS OF PERCEPTION WERE CLEANSED EVERY THING WOULD APPEAR TO MAN AS IT IS, INFINITE."

**?**

# A DENTIST INVENTED THE ELECTRIC CHAIR

In France, it used to be illegal to sell dolls with non-human faces. ET dolls, for example, were banned.

*Sheep are capable of remembering up to 50 familiar faces and remembering them for about two years. They can even recognize other sheep from pictures!*

**?**

ONE IN 2,000 BABIES ARE BORN
WITH ONE OR MORE TEETH.

## There are more bacteria in your mouth than people in the world.

TEXAS HORNED LIZARDS CAN
SHOOT BLOOD OUT OF THE
CORNERS OF THEIR EYES.

ASTRONAUTS ABOARD THE INTERNATIONAL
SPACE STATION WITNESS 15 SUNSETS AND
SUNRISES EVERYDAY; AN AVERAGE OF ONE
EVERY 45 MINUTES.

# ?

MCDONALD'S IS
THE LARGEST TOY
DISTRIBUTOR IN THE
WORLD. BY FAR.

NAPOLEON CONSTRUCTED HIS
BATTLE PLANS IN A SANDBOX

In marshy areas French
shepherds traditionally
walked around on stilts.

EVEN A SMALL AMOUNT OF ALCOHOL
WILL MAKE A SCORPION STING ITSELF
VIOLENTLY. LUCKILY, THEY ARE IMMUNE
TO THEIR OWN VENOM.

nkeys like banana daiquiris.

## Donkeys kill more people than aircraft crashes.

PROPORTIONAL TO WEIGHT, HUMANS ARE STRONGER THAN HORSES.

ALLIGATORS, KANGAROOS, EMUS AND PENGUINS CANNOT MOVE BACKWARDS.

'FOR SALE: BABY SHOES, NEVER WORN', IS THE ENTIRETY OF THE SHORTEST NOVEL EVER PUBLISHED.

THE SANSKRIT WORD FOR "WAR" MEANS 'DESIRE FOR MORE COWS.'

**?**

# MARTIAN SUNSETS ARE BLUE

THE WORDS 'SACRILEGIOUS' AND 'RELIGION' HAVE TOTALLY UNRELATED ORIGINS.

MOST TROPICAL MARINE FISH COULD SURVIVE IN A TANK FILLED WITH HUMAN BLOOD.

*Cleopatra married two of her brothers.*

THE WHISKERS ON CATFISH ARE CALLED BARBELLS.

**?**

*A full moon is nine times brighter than a half moon.*

IN 19TH-CENTURY BRITAIN ATTEMPTED
SUICIDE WAS PUNISHABLE BY HANGING.

OVEREATING REDUCES YOUR ABILITY TO HEAR

BLUEBIRDS CANNOT SEE THE COLOUR
BLUE. IN FACT, OWLS ARE THE ONLY
BIRDS THAT CAN DETECT BLUE LIGHT.

SIR ISAAC NEWTON
INVENTED
THE CAT FLAP.

**?**

Humans tell their first lie around age two.

*At any one time 0.7% of the world's population is drunk.*

'GOODBYE' COMES FROM 'GOD BE WITH YOU'.

FEBRUARY 1865 IS THE ONLY MONTH IN RECORDED HISTORY IN WHICH THERE WAS NO FULL MOON.

*St Isador of Castille is the Patron Saint of the Internet.*

A GROUP OF KANGAROOS IS CALLED

# A MOB

**?**

'*Able was I ere I saw Elba*'
*is a palindrome
written by Napoleon.*

RABBITS AND RATS CANNOT VOMIT.

ELEPHANTS, RHINOS, HIPPOS AND
SLOTHS ARE THE ONLY MAMMALS
THAT CAN'T JUMP.

*Children grow fastest in the spring.*

# LIVING PEOPLE CANNOT APPEAR ON US STAMPS

'ONE THOUSAND' IS THE FIRST NUMBER SPELLED WITH THE LETTER 'A'.

ALBERT EINSTEIN AND CHARLES DARWIN BOTH MARRIED THEIR FIRST COUSINS.

## The Bible is the most shoplifted book in the world.

THE EIFFEL TOWER ALWAYS LEANS AWAY FROM THE SUN. THIS IS BECAUSE HEAT EXPANDS THE METAL.

**?**

COWS CAN WALK UPSTAIRS,
BUT NOT DOWN.

PASTING A BRITISH POSTAGE
STAMP UPSIDE-DOWN IS
TECHNICALLY TREASON.

*In France, it is forbidden to call
a pig 'Napoleon.'*

ASTRONAUTS BECOME 5-8CM
TALLER IN SPACE.

HUMANS ARE BORN WITH FULLY-
GROWN EYES, BUT THE NOSE AND EARS
NEVER STOP GROWING.

**?**

*Tom Cruise was voted 'Least Likely to Succeed' in High School.*

Male Hospital patients fall out of bed twice as often as female patients.

An early draft of Steinbeck's 'Of Mice and Men' was eaten by his dog

*The shape of bubbles in beer foam is properly called 'orthotetrachidecahedrons'.*

**?**

QUEEN ANTS CAN LIVE UP
TO 45 YEARS.

*The longest recorded time between two
twins being born is 87 days.*

THE HUNDRED YEARS WAR LASTED
FOR 116 YEARS.

THE NAME 'WENDY'
WAS INVENTED BY
J.M. BARRIE,
THE AUTHOR OF
PETER PAN.

ARMADILLOS CAN BE
HOUSE-TRAINED.

## Mount Everest moves about 10cm north every year.

FOR SIX WEEKS DURING WWII A REINDEER
CALLED POLLYANNA LIVED ABOARD THE BRITISH
SUBMARINE HMS TRIDENT.

CENOSILLICAPHOBIA
IS THE FEAR OF AN
EMPTY GLASS

ABOUT ONE IN 20 PEOPLE
HAVE AN EXTRA RIB.

SINCE 1945, ALL BRITISH
TANKS HAVE BEEN EQUIPPED
TO MAKE TEA.

*You consume a tenth of a
calorie when you
lick a stamp.*

THE FINNISH WORD
'SAIPPUAKIVIKAUPPIAS'
(SOAPSTONE SELLER) IS THE LONGEST
PALINDROME IN ANY LANGUAGE.

*The lighter was invented before the match.*

Giraffes and rats can last longer without water than camels.

A blue whale's tongue weighs more than an adult elephant.

*Antarctica has two ATMs. Since they're only serviced once every two years, one of the machines serves mainly as a backup.*

we share 70%
OF OUR DNA
WITH SLUGS

*It snowed in the Sahara desert on the 18th February 1979.*

VODKA' IS RUSSIAN FOR 'WATER OF LIFE', WITH THE LITERAL TRANSLATION BEING 'LITTLE WATER'.

ALTHOUGH THE ABILITY TO LICK YOUR OWN ELBOW IS RARE, THE GUINNESS BOOK OF WORLD RECORDS HAVE RELEASED THIS STATEMENT ON THIS ISSUE: "BEING ABLE TO LICK YOUR OWN ELBOW IS NOT, IN ANY SENSE, A WORLD RECORD. IF YOU'RE ONE OF THE RARE FEW WHO CAN LICK YOUR ELBOW, SAVE IT FOR THE WATER COOLER."

*A survey reported that 12% of Americans thought that Joan of Arc was Noah's wife.*

BRAZIL IS NAMED AFTER THE BRAZIL NUT, NOT THE OTHER WAY AROUND.

THE WORD 'HAMSTER' COMES FROM THE GERMAN 'TO HOARD'.

EVERY BEARDED US PRESIDENT HAS BEEN A REPUBLICAN.

THE PRACTICE OF WATCHING PEOPLE EAT,
IN THE HOPE OF BEING OFFERED SOME FOOD,
IS CALLED

'GROAKING'.

*Donkeys sink in quicksand,*
*but mules don't.*

THE OLDEST LIGHT BULB HAD BEEN
RUNNING SINCE 1901.

A FOETUS ACQUIRES
FINGERPRINTS AT
THREE MONTHS.

**?**

THE EARTH IS THE ONLY PLANET IN THE SOLAR SYSTEM NOT NAMED AFTER A GOD.

SPIDERS' SILK IS STRONGER THAN STEEL.

ALL THE COAL, OIL AND GAS ON EARTH COULD ONLY FUEL THE SUN FOR A COUPLE OF DAYS.

HALF OF ALL BANK ROBBERIES OCCUR ON A FRIDAY

**?**

*In the Czech Republic, beer is often cheaper than Coca-Cola or coffee.*

# THE USA PRODUCES MORE TOBACCO THAN WHEAT.

*The UK eats more baked beans than the rest of the world combined.*

A BALL OF GLASS WILL BOUNCE HIGHER THAN A BALL OF RUBBER.

# ?

# YOUR HEAVIEST ORGAN IS YOUR SKIN

*Only three english words begin with 'dw': 'dwell', 'dwindle' and 'dwarf'.*

THE GHOST CLUB, THE OLDEST ORGANISATION INVESTIGATING THE PARANORMAL AND SUPERNATURAL, HAS HAD DISTINGUISHED MEMBERS, INCLUDING CHARLES DICKEN, W.B.YEATS, SIR ARTHUR CONAN DOYLE AND SIEGRIED SASSOON.

Around 1,000 people a year are injured by wheelbarrows in the UK each year.

**?**

BEER IS THE THIRD MOST POPULAR DRINK IN THE WORLD, AFTER WATER AND TEA.

## 'Cervisiam, sodes!' is how you order a beer in Latin.

**The minimum daily wage in ancient Egypt was two containers of beer a day.**

DUE TO THEIR SIMILAR PROTEIN COMPOSITION, BLOOD MAKES A GOOD EGG SUBSTITUTE IN BAKING AND ICE-CREAM MAKING.

CATS CANNOT TASTE SWEET THINGS

**?**

THE FIRST US MARINES' RECRUITING STATION WAS IN A BAR.

MEADOPHILY IS THE STUDY OF BEER BOTTLE LABELS

IN 2010, BOTTLES OF BEER FOUND IN A 200 YEAR-OLD SHIPWRECK WERE STILL DRINKABLE.

THE CHESS TERM 'CHECKMATE' COMES FROM A 14TH CENTURY ARABIC PHRASE, 'SHAH MAT', WHICH MEANS 'THE KING IS HELPLESS.'

*When you blush, your stomach lining also blushes.*

# ?

Vampire bats urinate whilst drinking blood to ensure they are not too heavy to fly.

*In 13th-century Norway some babies were baptised with beer.*

Frogs can't chew, and use their eyes to swallow. The eyes descend in the skull to help push food into the throat.

*Scaphism, or 'the boats', was an ancient Persian type of execution in which the victim was covered in honey and tied in between two boats whilst insects ate him alive.*

**?**

Live ants are served at 'The Noma' restaurant in Denmark, and are said to taste of lemongrass.

7 MILLION PINTS OF GUINNESS ARE DRUNK WORLDWIDE EVERY DAY.

MODERN SINGING BIRTHDAY CARDS HAVE MORE COMPUTING POWER THAN THE ALLIED FORCES IN 1945.

BEER CONTAINS ALMOST ALL OF THE MINERALS ESSENTIAL TO HUMAN SURVIVAL.

**?**

INDONESIA IS THE WORLD'S LARGEST
EXPORTER OF EDIBLE FROGS.

19TH-CENTURY BOOKS HAVE
BEEN DISCOVERED BOUND IN
HUMAN SKIN.

DEAD PIGEONS, URINE, AND TOBACCO
WERE AMONG THE MOST POPULAR
'CURES' FOR THE PLAGUE IN
17TH-CENTURY LONDON.

*If a starfish is cut into
separate pieces, each piece will
grow into a new starfish.*

**?**

TURKEY VULTURES FAVOR SEA-LION
EXCREMENT OVER ALL OTHER FOODS.

# 75% of house dust is made up of dead skin flakes.

JOAN OF ARC WAS BURNT A TOTAL OF THREE
TIMES TO PREVENT ANYONE STEALING HER
ASHES AS RELICS

THE WINNER OF THE 2013 NATHAN'S
HOT DOG EATING CONTEST CONSUMED 69
HOTDOGS IN 10 MINUTES.

**?**

Sea cucumbers can vomit out their internal organs to confuse predators while they escape.

Your feet produce 21.5 litres of sweat each year.

*Vending machines installed in Istanbul dispense food and water to dogs in exchange for recyclable plastic bottles.*

In 1871, lawyer Clement Vallandigham accidentally shot and killed himself demonstrating to an Ohio jury how a victim may possibly have shot himself.

**?**

*Without saliva, your mouth would be so acidic that your teeth would dissolve.*

PERUVIANS EAT 65 MILLION GUINEA PIGS EVERY YEAR.

TWO PLANES, WHICH COLLIDED IN AUSTRALIA IN 1940, REMAINED JOINED AND LANDED SAFELY WITH NO LOSS OF LIFE.

APPLE PIPS CONTAIN CYANIDE

HORSE-FLAVOURED ICE CREAM IS SOLD IN JAPAN.

# PEA PLANTS CAN GROW INSIDE A HUMAN LUNG

IN 1842, THE PRESIDENT OF MEXICO HELD A STATE FUNERAL FOR HIS SEVERED LEG.

*Ken Edwards holds the record for eating 36 cockroaches in one minute.*

BEARS WERE USED TO TEST
EJECTOR SEATS BY THE US
DURING THE COLD WAR.

**?**

IN 18TH-CENTURY ENGLAND, A POPULAR COUGH MEDICINE WAS MADE FROM SNAILS BOILED IN TEA.

*A group of 24 rabbits set loose in Australia grew to a population of 10 billion in 67 years.*

CANNED CATERPILLARS ARE AVAILABLE IN MOST MEXICAN SUPERMARKETS.

*Haggis has been officially banned in the US since 1989.*

**?**

IN THE MIDDLE AGES, MOST
MINOR OPERATIONS WERE
CARRIED OUT BY BARBERS.

PATTERNS LEFT ON THE SKIN OF
LIGHTING STRIKE VICTIMS ARE CALLED
'LICHTENBERG FIGURES.'

SEVERED HUMAN FINGERTIPS
CAN GROW BACK NATURALLY

90% OF THE WILDLIFE OF MADAGASCAR IS
UNIQUE TO THE ISLAND.

**?**

# A FIREFLY'S LIGHT SHINES FROM ITS ANUS.

EUROPE IS THE ONLY CONTINENT WITHOUT A DESERT

IN NORTH KOREA, WOMEN MUST CHOSE ONE OF 18 OFFICIALLY SANCTIONED HAIRSTYLES. MEN HAVE TEN CHOICES.

*Americans collectively eat roughly 18 acres of pizza every day.*

# MOST LIPSTICK CONTAINS FISH SCALES

## BARBIE'S FULL NAME IS
### BARBARA MILLICENT ROBERTS.

A POPULAR GAME IN THE MIDDLE AGES WAS TO TIE YOUR HANDS BEHIND YOUR BACK THEN TRY TO BEAT A CAT TO DEATH WITH YOUR HEAD.

## GRAPES EXPLODE IN THE MICROWAVE

**?**

PIRATES BELIEVED THAT WEARING EARRINGS IMPROVED THEIR EYESIGHT

UNDERPANTS ARE AVAILABLE IN SOME JAPANESE VENDING MACHINES.

*The potato was shunned in parts of 17th-century Europe because it was believed to cause leprosy.*

DEMAND FOR PIANOS HAS DROPPED SO RADICALLY THAT YOU CAN NOW ADOPT ONE.

**?**

A toilet at the back of a monastery or convent is called 'the necessarium'.

# President Barak Obama knows sign language.

THE FIRST SILICONE BREAST IMPLANT PROCEDURE WAS PERFORMED ON A DOG CALLED ESMERELDA.

ALCOHOL IS CONSIDERED A PERFORMANCE-ENHANCING DRUG IN COMPETITIVE SHOOTING.

**?**

# CAMELS HAVE THREE EYELIDS PER EYE

A PIGEON'S BONES WEIGH LESS THAN ITS FEATHERS.

*The world record for swallowing sausages is seven in one minute.*

ACCORDING TO ASTRONAUTS, SPACE SMELLS LIKE SEARED STEAK, HOT METAL, AND WELDING FUMES.

IN OHIO, IT IS ILLEGAL
TO GET A FISH DRUNK.

**?**

BEES CAN DETECT
EXPLOSIVES.

*Barbie has had 125 different careers
since 1959.*

IT TAKES FORTY MINUTES TO
HARD-BOIL AN OSTRICH EGG.

IT IS ILLEGAL TO ENTER THE BRITISH
HOUSES OF PARLIAMENT WHILST WEARING
A SUIT OR ARMOUR. IT IS ALSO ILLEGAL
TO DIE IN THE HOUSES OF PARLIAMENT.
ALTHOUGH, IF YOU DO, YOU ARE ENTITLED
TO A STATE FUNERAL.

**?**

# ADULTS HAVE FEWER BONES THAN BABIES

Pregnant women most commonly crave pickles and peanut butter.

*In mourning for their cats, ancient Egyptians shaved off their eyebrows.*

IT IS POSSIBLE TO ABUSE NUTMEG AS A HALLUCINOGENIC SUBSTANCE IN LARGE ENOUGH DOSES.

**?**

# GRASSHOPPERS
### are reported to taste of beef.

*In Samoa, it is illegal to forget your wife's birthday.*

THERE ARE MORE
POSSIBLE ORDERINGS
OF A DECK OF CARDS
THAN THERE HAVE BEEN
SECONDS SINCE
THE BIG BANG.

# ?

## In 1647, the British Long Parliament banned Christmas.

During World War II, an exploding toilet was responsible for sinking a German submarine.

The very first YouTube video, uploaded on 5th May 2005, is called 'Me at the Zoo".

# ?

## AVOCADOS are fatal to parrots.

snails can crawl along the edge of a razor without cutting themselves.

### `Charles the Mad`, a 14th-century King of France, thought he was made of grass.

In 1518, it was reported that a woman danced herself to death. The phenomenon apparently spread to 400 other people and became known as the 'Dancing Plague'.

# COWS
## HAVE BEST FRIENDS

**?**

LOUIS XIII OF FRANCE USED TO HOLD MEETINGS WHILST SITTING ON THE TOILET.

*Octopi have been known to eat their own tentacles under stress.*

THE ARMADILLO IS ONE OF THE ONLY ANIMALS, APART FROM HUMANS, THAT CAN SUFFER FROM LEPROSY.

IN QUEENSLAND, AUSTRALIA, YOU CAN ONLY KEEP RABBITS IF YOU RUN AN ANIMAL TESTING LAB, OR HAVE A MAGICIAN'S LICENSE.

# ?

## *Hot water freezes faster than cold water.*

BREAKING WIND IS A BOOKABLE OFFENSE IN FOOTBALL.

IN THE NETHERLANDS, SANTA CLAUS BUNDLES NAUGHTY CHILDREN INTO A SACK AND TAKES THEM TO SPAIN.

## NAKED RAMBLING IS LEGAL IN SWITZERLAND.

**?**

TONGUE PRINTS ARE UNIQUE, JUST
LIKE FINGERPRINTS.

IN 896 AD, POPE FORMOSUS WAS
PUT ON TRIAL DESPITE BEING
DEAD AT THE TIME.

During World War II, an Italian
newspaper claimed that the Loch Ness
Monster had been killed in the Blitz.

IN THE UK, IT IS ILLEGAL TO BE DRUNK
WHILST IS THE POSSESSION OF A FIREARM,
HORSE, OR STEAM ENGINE.

# ?

ASTON VILLA FC WAS FOUNDED BY
CRICKETERS LOOKING TO KEEP FIT
OVER THE WINTER MONTHS

BEFORE WHISTLES WERE INTRODUCED
IN 1878, FOOTBALL REFEREES WAVED
HANDKERCHIEFS TO HALT PLAY.

*The western lowland gorilla's scientific*
*name is "Gorilla Gorilla Gorilla."*
*This is its genus, species and sub-species.*

ONE OF THE TOP-DIVISION FOOTBALL
TEAMS IN GHANA IS CALLED
"THE MYSTERIOUS DWARFS".

**?**

THE CHANCES OF GETTING TWO
HOLES-IN-ONE IN A ROUND OF GOLF
ARE 67 MILLION TO ONE.

## George W. Bush proposed to his wife on a miniature golf course.

HARPO MARX AND GEORGE BURNS WERE
ADMONISHED FOR NOT WEARING SHIRTS
WHILST PLAYING GOLF ON A HOT SUMMER'S
DAY. THEY RESPONDED BY TAKING THEIR
TROUSERS OFF AS WELL.

*The world's shortest war was between England
and Zanzibar, and lasted 45 minutes.*

?

BULLET—PROOF VESTS, WINDSHIELD WIPERS,
AND LASER PRINTERS
WERE ALL INVENTED BY WOMEN.

MUD-THROWING WAS AN OFFICIAL
OLYMPIC SPORT IN 1904.

REASONS FOR ADMISSION TO AN ASYLUM IN
WEST VIRGINIA BETWEEN 1864 AND 1889
INCLUDED: 'IMAGINARY FEMALE TROUBLE',
'NOVEL READING', 'BAD WHISKEY', AND
'SNUFF EATING FOR TWO YEARS'.

*In 2012, a Dutch artist became the first
person to produce a real cloud indoors.*

**?**

THE WORD 'TOYOTA' MEANS
'BOUNTIFUL RICE FIELD'
IN JAPANESE.

*'Bromidrosis'*
*is the scientific term for*
*sweaty feet.*

IN SOME PARTS OF NORTHERN CHILE, IT
HAS NOT RAINED FOR 400 YEARS.

THE FRENCH CALL APRIL FOOL'S DAY,
'APRIL FISH DAY'.

*Only domestic dogs bark. Barking has*
*never been observed in wild dogs.*

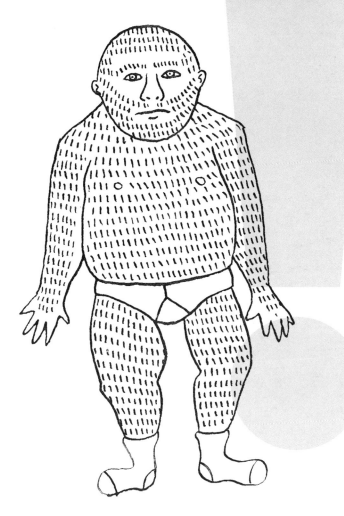

THE WORLD'S HAIRIEST MAN IS YU
ZHENHUAN FROM CHINA. HIS BODY
IS 96% COVERED IN LONG HAIR

# ?

*Charlie Chaplin once came third in a Charlie Chaplin look-alike contest.*

THE MONA LISA USED TO HANG IN NAPOLEON'S BEDROOM.

THE STATUE OF LIBERTY WEARS SIZE 879 SHOES.

IN 2013, A TUNNEL IN NORWAY WAS CLOSED BECAUSE IT WAS TOTALLY FILLED WITH BURNING GOATS' CHEESE.

**?**

THE BEATLES SONG 'A DAY IN THE LIFE'
FEATURES A HIGH-PITCHED WHISTLE
ONLY AUDIBLE TO DOGS.

ON MERCURY AND VENUS
DAYS ARE LONGER THAN YEARS

THE FIRST WORD SPOKEN ON THE MOON WAS

'OKAY'.

CONTRARY TO POPULAR BELIEF, GOLDFISH CAN
RETAIN MEMORIES FOR SEVERAL MONTHS,
AS OPPOSED TO ONLY THREE SECONDS.

**?**

*Apart from humans, black lemurs are the only primates that can have blue eyes.*

# STARFISH DON'T HAVE BRAINS OR BLOOD.

## OSTRICHES URINATE ON THEIR LEGS TO KEEP COOL.

### MCDONALD'S SELL 75 HAMBURGERS EVERY SECOND.

**?**

A lake in Tanzania turns unwitting animals to stone, due to extremely high pH levels.

*Attila the Hun died of a nosebleed on his wedding night.*

BABIES ARE BORN WITHOUT KNEECAPS

THE FIRST SONG TO BE SUNG IN SPACE WAS 'HAPPY BIRTHDAY'.

**?**

# BEES HAVE FIVE EYES

AL CAPONE'S BUSINESS CARD DESCRIBED HIM AS A SECOND-HAND FURNITURE DEALER.

IGUANAS SNEEZE MORE OFTEN, AND MORE PRODUCTIVELY THAN ANY OTHER ANIMAL.

THE AVERAGE HUMAN BODY CONTAINS ENOUGH IRON TO MAKE A 3-INCH NAIL.

*Elvis Presley's middle name is misspelled on his gravestone.*

*Woolly Mammoths still roamed the Earth when the Pyramids were built.*

**?**

# GIRAFFES ARE THE ONLY ANIMALS BORN WITH HORNS

Saint Valentine is the patron saint of both lovers and beekeepers.

## The Mona Lisa has no eyebrows.

Princess Anne was the only athlete not obliged to undergo a gender check in the 1972 Olympics.

SWEAT HAS NO NATURAL ODOUR

**?**

A mayoral election in Ecuador was once won by a foot powder.

In Florida, it is prohibited for divorced women and widows to parachute on Sundays.

About 50 double espressos amount to a lethal dose of caffeine.

The Tate Gallery in London is named after the inventor of the sugar cube.

*Gorillas are vegetarians.*

# ?

UNDER HENRY VIII, BOILING CONVICTS TO DEATH WAS A LEGITIMATE FORM OF PUNISHMENT.

*Laughing is considered an aggressive gesture by parrots.*

RATHER THAN HIRING CHIMNEY-SWEEPS, POORER VICTORIANS PUSHED LIVE GEESE DOWN THEIR CHIMNEYS.

THE 'IMMORTAL JELLYFISH' (OR TURRITOPSIS DOHRNII), CAN REVERT BACK TO A POLYP, AND REPEAT THIS PROCESS INDEFINITELY. IT IS THE ONLY CREATURE CONSIDERED TO BE BIOLOGICALLY IMMORTAL.

?

THOMAS EDISON PROPOSED TO HIS
SECOND WIFE IN MORSE CODE

IN 1929, WOMEN WERE DISCOVERED
TO BE "PERSONS" IN CANADA.

*A blind chameleon can still change color
for camouflage.*

APPLES, ADDERS AND APRONS USED TO
BE CALLED 'NAPPLES', 'NADDERS' AND
'NAPRONS'. PHRASES LIKE 'A NAPPLE'
WERE MISHEARD AS 'AN APPLE', AND
THE WORDS GRADUALLY CHANGED.

**?**

## The average life expectancy of a toilet is 50 years.

EXCEPT FOR IDENTICAL TWINS, EVERYBODY HAS A UNIQUE BODY ODOUR.

## CDS KEPT IN THE FRIDGE PRODUCE BETTER SOUND QUALITY.

AS WELL AS DIAGNOSING BROKEN BONES, X-RAYS HAVE REVEALED ITEMS SUCH AS GRENADES, SWORDS, CHAIR LEGS, BEDSPRINGS, FORKS AND RUBBER DUCKS, LODGED INSIDE PEOPLE.

**?**

In the 14th century, a French pig was executed for eating an infant.

The 19th of September is International Talk Like a Pirate Day.

*Not all of your taste buds are on your tongue.*

The Ayam Cemani chicken is totally black, except for its blood. It has black plumage, black skin, black bones, black organs, black meat, black nails, beak and tongue.

*King George II died as a result of falling off the toilet.*

# THE FILM 'PSYCHO' FEATURES THE WORLD'S FIRST ON-SCREEN TOILET.

'YELLING AT YOUR SHOES' AND 'TECHNICOLOR YAWNING' ARE EUPHEMISMS FOR VOMITING.

TARDIGRADES, OR 'WATER BEARS', ARE THE ONLY ANIMALS THOUGHT TO BE ABLE TO SURVIVE IN THE VACUUM OF SPACE. THIS IS BECAUSE THEY ARE UNIQUELY TOLERANT TO RADIATION AND DESICCATION.

**?**

HONEY, DRIED RICE, SALT AND SUGAR ARE THE ONLY RAW FOODS THAT WONT GO OFF. EVER.

LOBSTERS URINATE FROM THEIR FACES.

## *Coca-Cola would be green without the added coloring.*

ADOLF HITLER WAS NAMED TIME MAGAZINE'S 'MAN OF THE YEAR' IN 1938, AND NOMINATED FOR THE NOBEL PEACE PRIZE IN 1939.

# ?

Otter couples hold hands while they sleep, so that they don't drift apart.

*A penguin was once knighted in Norway. His full title is 'Colonel-in-Chief Sir Nils Olav'.*

Rabbit show-jumping, or 'Kaninhopping', is a competitive event in Sweden.

Dung beetles use the Milky Way to navigate.

*Sharks are immune to cancer.*

**?**

*More Monopoly money than real currency is printed each year.*

THOUSANDS OF NEW TREES ARE PLANTED EACH YEAR WHEN SQUIRRELS FORGET WHERE THEY'VE HIDDEN THEIR ACORNS.

REINDEER CAN'T PEE AND WALK AT THE SAME TIME.

STRAWBERRIES AREN'T BERRIES, BUT BANANAS AND AVOCADOS ARE.

*Crocodiles are cannibals.*

**?**

## Rats laugh when tickled.

THERE IS A POSITIVE CORRELATION BETWEEN THE AVERAGE AMOUNT OF CHOCOLATE A COUNTRY CONSUMES AND THE NUMBER OF NOBEL LAUREATES THAT COUNTRY HAS PRODUCED.

IN ALASKA, IT IS ILLEGAL TO LOOK AT A MOOSE FROM AN AIRPLANE.

THERE ARE MORE TELEPHONES THAN PEOPLE IN WASHINGTON D.C.

SHAKESPEARE IS RESPONSIBLE FOR INVENTING 1700 ENGLISH WORDS, INCLUDING 'ELBOW', 'LONELY', 'OBSCENE', 'UNCOMFORTABLE' AND 'GOSSIP'.

# THE ORIGINAL VOICE ACTORS FOR MICKEY AND MINNIE MOUSE WERE MARRIED.

**?**

TERMITES EAT THROUGH WOOD
TWICE AS FAST WHEN LISTENING
TO ROCK MUSIC.

In Japan, it is considered good
luck to have a sumo wrestler
make your baby cry.

Between 1900 and 1920 Tug-of-War was
an Olympic sport.

GOOGLE WAS
ORIGINALLY CALLED
'BACKRUB'.

# ?

*Astronomers estimate that 275 million new stars are born every day.*

In vermont, women must have written permission from their husbands in order to wear false teeth.

CATS CAN BE ALLERGIC TO HUMANS

ONLY WOMEN CAN PUT THEIR WHOLE FISTS IN THEIR MOUTHS.

**?**

ON THE 1ST SEPTEMBER 2004, ILKER YILMAZ, FROM TURKEY, SQUIRTED MILK FROM HIS EYE A DISTANCE OF 9 FEET AND 2 INCHES.

IN NIGERIA, SUPERSTITION WARNS AGAINST KISSING BABIES ON THE LIPS. SUPPOSEDLY, IT WILL CAUSE THEM TO DROOL AS ADULTS.

*In Denmark, if you are unmarried by the time you turn 25, it is traditional for your friends to assault you with powdered cinnamon.*

**?**

JEF VAN DIJCK HOLDS THE RECORD FOR WEARING THE MOST T-SHIRTS AT ONE TIME. ON 24TH APRIL 2008, HE MANAGED TO DON 227 T-SHIRTS.

*Since there is no wind on the moon, footprints left by astronauts could last for up to 10 million years.*

IN AUSTRIA, FINGER-PULLING, OR 'FINGERHAKELN', IS A FIERCELY COMPETITIVE SPORT. FINGER-ATHLETES AIM TO DRAG THEIR OPPONENT ACROSS THE TABLE BY THEIR FINGER.

YOU CAN'T HUM WHILST HOLDING YOUR NOSE.

# In Welsh folklore, fairies traveled around riding corgis.

THERE ARE MORE FAKE FLAMINGOS IN THE WORLD THAN REAL FLAMINGOS

THE UNIVERSE MIGHT BE A HOLOGRAM. SOME SCIENTISTS SUGGEST THAT OUR PERCEPTION OF THE UNIVERSE IS A THREE-DIMENSIONAL HALLUCINATION WHICH WE ARE EXPERIENCING FROM A TWO-DIMENSIONAL EXISTENCE.

# ?

## PRAIRIE DOGS KISS HELLO

It rains diamonds on Saturn and Jupiter.

*The population of Mars consists entirely of robots.*

90% OF YOUR BODY MASS IS LITERALLY STARDUST. THIS IS BECAUSE ALL THE ELEMENTS EXCEPT HYDROGEN AND HELIUM ARE FUSED IN STARS.

**?**

IF YOU ARE OVER 45, THE WORLD'S POPULATION HAS DOUBLED IN YOUR LIFETIME.

*Leonardo da Vinci could simultaneously draw with one hand and write with the other.*

THERE'S A PLANET (KNOWN AS HD189733B) WHERE IT RAINS GLASS.

DEAD BATTERIES BOUNCE; FULL BATTERIES DON'T.

**?**

Duelling is legal in Paraguay, but only so long as both parties are registered blood donors.

THERE ARE MORE POSSIBLE CONFIGURATIONS IN A CHESS GAME THAN ATOMS IN THE UNIVERSE.

BEER WAS CLASSIFIED AS A SOFT DRINK IN RUSSIA UNTIL 2011.

TWO-THIRDS OF PEOPLE ON EARTH HAVE NEVER SEEN SNOW.

**?**

# A hummingbird weighs less than a penny.

YOU are 1% SHORTER IN THE EVENING THAN WHEN YOU WOKE UP.

FRENCH WAS THE OFFICIAL LANGUAGE OF ENGLAND FOR OVER 600 YEARS.

**The chance of dying on your way to buy a lottery ticket is greater than your chance of winning.**

ALTHOUGH THE TONGUE IS NOT THE STRONGEST MUSCLE IN YOUR BODY, IF IT WERE THE SIZE OF AN ELEPHANT'S TRUNK, IT COULD UPROOT TREES.

MALE MICE SING TO
WOO FEMALES.